COLLABORATING FOR CONNECTION AS A COUPLE

COLLABORATIVE ATTACHMENT SYSTEMS THERAPY

KYLE N. WEIR, PHD, LMFT
CALIFORNIA STATE UNIVERSITY - FRESNO
WORKBOOK 1 FOR COUPLES

Copyright © 2021 by Kyle N. Weir, PhD, LMFT

Published by Finegold Creek Press, LLC

P.O. Box 1272

Washington, UT 84780

All rights reserved.

No part of this book may be reproduced in any form or by any electronic or mechanical means, including information storage and retrieval systems, without written permission from the author, except for the use of brief quotations in a book review.

The information in this book is for informational and educational purposes and is not intended to be a substitute for professional medical or therapeutic advice, diagnosis, or treatment.

For my wife Allison -
Who has been my partner in collaboration, connection, and attachment
through the years.

COLLABORATING FOR CONNECTION AS A COUPLE:

COLLABORATIVE ATTACHMENT SYSTEMS THERAPY

Workbook 1 for Couples

CONTENTS

Introduction	ix
1. Chapter One - Preparations: Pairing with Your Perceptions (and Pairing Against the Problems)	1
2. Chapter Two - Collaboration	7
3. Chapter Three - Attachment: Theory	18
4. Chapter Four - Systems as a Way to Rebuild Relationships	27
5. Chapter Five - Therapy: A Planned Interlude to Address Your Issues and Challenges in the Context of CAST	44
Continuing Therapy with Collaborative Attachment Systems Therapy	49
Notes	51
About the Author	55

INTRODUCTION

Congratulations! You are seeking help. That is the first step towards resolving issues in your relationship. The fact that you are seeking information about marriage and other forms of couples' relationships is a positive factor in your favor. With counseling, information, education, and your hard work toward changing patterns concerning both feelings and behaviors in your companionship, you can be very hopeful that the relationship you want is possible to achieve.

This workbook, along with the other two workbooks in the series, carries some basic assumptions:

1. That you are committed to work on your relationship with your partner.
2. That you are entering counseling with a competent marriage & family therapist (MFT), counselor, or other trained mental health professional with experience working with couples and families, alongside of the use of this and subsequent workbooks, preferably one trained in Collaborative Attachment Systems Therapy (CAST).
3. That you are willing to do homework between clinical and

ix

INTRODUCTION

psychoeducational sessions to strive to make changes in
both yourself and your relationship.

4. That you are seeking to work together with your partner in
   a collaborative effort to be more closely connected and
   safely secure in your attachment to your spouse or partner.

5. That there aren't major issues that need to be addressed
   first before couples counseling can be effective. For
   example, if your spouse or partner has a substance abuse
   addiction, that issue must be treated first before couples
   therapy work will be effective. If there is intimate partner
   violence or domestic violence in the home, couples therapy
   as outlined in these workbooks should not be attempted
   until after separate individual and group counseling has
   occurred to end the cycle of violence in the family. Also, if
   severe mental illness (like psychosis, personality disorders,
   severe psychopathology) or other disabilities are impairing
   functioning, those must be addressed before couples
   therapy can be attempted.

As you utilize these workbooks, pay attention to the feelings,
thoughts, and behaviors that arise. These are the three areas of change
for all effective therapies. If you can change how you think, feel, and
do things in your relationship, you can change almost anything for the
better. The Collaborative Attachment Systems Therapy (CAST)
approach is built on the integration of several evidenced-based best
practices in couples therapy. Integrating the best of the best models of
couples therapy is the fundamental reason why CAST is such an
effective model for couples treatment. It builds off of the work of
several notable researchers and practitioners with high rates of
success and combines them into one powerful approach to heal a
couple's relationship.

Additionally, these workbooks presuppose that principles that
make couples successful and happy can be learned. While the applica-
tion of these principles may be unique to you and your relationship,
the principles generally work for most people. But if you find that you

x

INTRODUCTION

have to modify or accommodate something in a workbook for your unique circumstances, talk with your therapist or counselor about how to do that. The structure of Collaborative Attachment Systems Therapy (CAST) is designed to spend about the first 20 minutes or so of a counseling session talking about the psycho-educational principles of a chapter in these workbooks and then the remainder of the time is devoted to how to apply the information to your relationship.

We recognize that a "one-size-fits-all" or "cookie-cutter" approach to counseling is not likely to be effective. In fact, our model addresses marital counseling primarily (since the numerical majority of couple's sessions in the United States do involve legally married heterosexual persons) but presents modifications to our approach for pre-marital counseling and cohabiting couples (both heterosexual and homosexual). Therapy tailored and designed to your relationship is our ultimate goal. We may present in generalities and note where exceptions and modifications are usually necessary (for premarital or cohabiting couples), but we hope that your therapist and you can collaboratively work to further mold the information to your unique couple-hood.

Finally, we'd like to end this introductory section with some definitions of key terms we will be using throughout these workbooks.

- **Collaboration** – Collaboration literally means *co-laboring* or *working together*. The hallmark of successful marriages and other couple's relationships is the ability to work well together as a team. Collaboration isn't the same as compromise, accommodation, competing, or avoiding. Collaboration involves high levels of communication, assertiveness, cooperation, sacrifice, and long-term commitment. When a couple feels like they can collaborate well with each other, they will draw strength, trust, cohesiveness, and determination as they face the tasks and challenges of life together. As collaboration builds, generally trust increases and resentment decreases in the relationship. Typically, couples find they collaborate best if they mutually serve some common higher purpose (for

xi

INTRODUCTION

example, raising a family together, serving God or one's
spiritual belief system, striving for mutually set goals, etc.).
Teamwork, friendship, and trust result from this
collaborative spirit in a couple's relationship.

- **Attachment** – Attachment has been studied by some of the
  greatest researchers of the 20th and 21st century in our field.
  It can be complex and nuanced, but for our purposes, we
  see attachment as one of our most basic human needs. It is
  the need to feel close, valued, and connected to important
  people (partners, parents, caregivers, and others) in a safe,
  secure way. Attachment is socially learned through our
  experiences. As we interact positively with significant
  people in our lives, we can build close, connected,
  meaningful, and secure attachments as the patterns of
  interaction demonstrate trust, dependability, consistency,
  accessibility, engagement, responsiveness, support, and
  mutual good will.

- **Systems** – People do not live in a vacuum. We live in
  relationships. The interactions between people have ripple
  effects. For example, if a spouse or partner has a bad day at
  work, when they come home their mood can affect their
  spouse, children, and everyone in the home. As therapists
  we have learned to trace the patterns of interactions in
  family systems and identify how changes can be made to
  maximize the positive ripple effects across the whole family.
  Most importantly, we have noticed something we call
  "circular causality" which simply means that interactions
  seem to spiral around and around causing predictable
  responses. Often family systems develop a balance at a
  miserable, unhappy level that the family members want to
  change, but don't know how to change. As therapists, we
  look to convert negative cycles into positive ones and strive
  to examine how miserably balanced systems that often fight
  these positive changes can be changed and rebalanced at
  healthier, happier levels.

xii

INTRODUCTION

- **Couple Identity Development** – Couple identity
  formation is one of the main developmental tasks each
  couple faces. It begins even before the marriage and changes
  throughout their life-cycle together. It involves re-orienting
  your lives, interests, social experiences, friendship
  networks, and activities from a single experience to a
  coupled experience. It is the shift from "me" to "we" – the
  reformulating yourself as "The Smith's" or the "Rodriguez's"
  (if your surname were Smith or Rodriguez) rather than
  "Bill" or "Maria." It is how you present yourselves to others
  as a couple and how you are known in your social network
  and community. This key task has many important
  implications that will be addressed later in this book.

Overview of the TRAIL to Love

Let me begin with a personal story. My first date with the girl who would grow to be my wife was at Disneyland in Anaheim, CA. We were very young teens at the time, but our love ripened and grew over the years. Eight years after that first date I proposed to Allison at, of all places, Disneyland, of course. We went on to marry (at the time of this writing we've been married over 27 years) and raise six great children. So, when I was at a conference in Anaheim in the "shadow" of the Matterhorn Mountain ride so to speak, my thoughts were drawn to love – how it grows, its elements, and how those elements are related. Walking to the conference an epiphany hit me about how love works. The key is that it develops through predictable phases that build on one another with deepening levels of vulnerability defining each phase. These phases mark a TRAIL to Love:

- Trust
- Regard
- Attachment
- Intimacy
- Love.

xiii

INTRODUCTION

Like most aspects of human development, this TRAIL to Love is *epigenetic*. Epigenetic literally means "above the beginning," but the part that is really relevant to understanding the development of love is that each phase uses and builds on the previous phase. So, to love, you first have to develop trust. Then, once trust is established you use trust to develop regard. Then you use trust and regard to develop attachment. Next, you use trust, regard, and attachment to create intimacy. Finally, you use trust, regard, attachment, and intimacy to build love. Each stage uses the abilities from previous stages to be successful at achieving the next. In the case of the TRAIL to Love it also involves deeper and deeper levels of vulnerability at each stage along the path.

Think of the TRAIL to Love like a five-tiered wedding cake:

Figure 1
The TRAIL Stages

When you take your first steps along the TRAIL to Love you stand on the first step – Trust. It takes great collaborative work to build trust, overcome barriers to trust, or rebuild trust if it has been lost. But with your collaborative efforts you successfully achieve a level of trust and a beginning sense of safety emerges or reemerges. From there you take the next step to Regard. With regard, things get personal. You find that you are more open to your partner, you feel a fondness for him or her, admiration increases, and they seem to preoccupy your thoughts more. At that point you are standing on both Regard and

xiv

INTRODUCTION

Trust drawing upon the successful achievements you've built as a couple together in both phases. To help your relationship grow to the next level, you have to increase your vulnerability and become attached to one another. At the Attachment phase you feel safe and secure in the relationship, you feel connected to one another, and your deepest desires to be cherished and valued by your partner flourish. At that point you are standing on the successful parts of your relationship: Attachment, Regard, and Trust. Using Trust, Regard, and Attachment you further deepen your vulnerability and develop Intimacy. In a previous book I defined intimacy as "the vulnerable sharing of one's self that is received with kindness and often mutually reciprocated."[1] By intimacy I mean all forms of intimacy – emotional, social, intellectual, spiritual, and physical (including sexual). With these deepened levels of Intimacy, Attachment, Regard, and Trust, your relationship can come to fruition in Love. Love is the deepest and most poignant human emotion. Love has many facets and forms. Love is not something we "fall" into or out of, but rather it is an emotion and connection we choose to give and receive (or not give or receive) through the collaborative efforts (or lack of effort) we decide to build into a relationship.

Homework

Each section or chapter in these workbooks will have a homework section for you, the couple, to complete before you meet with your therapist or counselor. Your homework for this introduction is this:

Each of you write down 2-3 things that motivates you to want to collaborate with your partner to build a better relationship.

_____

_____

_____

_____

_____

_____

INTRODUCTION

Without judging each other's responses, each of you write down where you think you are at on the TRAIL to Love. Also write down what you think is blocking you from taking the next step along the TRAIL to Love.

_____

_____

_____

_____

_____

_____

_____

Recommended Readings

Each section or chapter in these workbooks will have recommended readings. These are not required, but are offered as additional resources should you desire to study the topics related to the chapter or section in greater depth.

- Sue Johnson (2013). *Love Sense: The Revolutionary New Science of Romantic Relationships.* New York, NY: Little, Brown and Company.

CHAPTER ONE - PREPARATIONS: PAIRING WITH YOUR PERCEPTIONS (AND PAIRING AGAINST THE PROBLEMS)

*A*s you and your partner are beginning therapy with a therapist or counselor trained in the Collaborative Attachment Systems Therapy (CAST) approach, there are some initial preparations that need to be made to help you have the most successful outcome possible. It is important for each of you to develop a working therapeutic relationship with your therapist.

PLEASE WRITE down 2-3 things you would like the therapist to know about you individually:

Partner 1:

_____

_____

_____

Partner 2:

_____

_____

_____

. . .

KYLE N. WEIR, PHD, LMFT

ADDITIONALLY, what are the 2-3 things you want the therapist to know about your relationship?

PARTNER 1:

_____
_____
_____

PARTNER 2:

_____
_____
_____

ALSO, what strengths do you see in your relationship?
     Partner 1:

_____
_____
_____

PARTNER 2:

_____
_____
_____

FINALLY, what are 2-3 things you would like to know about your therapist (for example, education, specialized training, background working with couples, licensure details, etc.):

.

.   .   .

2

COLLABORATING FOR CONNECTION AS A COUPLE

PARTNER 1:

_____

_____

_____

PARTNER 2:

_____

_____

_____

ONE COMMON CONCERN couples often have when starting couples therapy is whether or not the therapist will be on the side of one partner or the other. In the beginning of the therapy process, some partners go to great lengths to "win" the therapist over to "their side" and view things "their way" over their partner's perspective. Rest assured that the CAST trained therapist has been taught to take a rather unique approach to this problem. While some therapy models want the therapist to be neutral and never take sides, the CAST therapist is trained to take *everyone's* side, meaning that the CAST therapist is trained to seek to fully understand *all* of the perspectives of the members of the family system. In the beginning of therapy, the therapist will be carefully seeking to fully understand your perspective and your partner's perspective. Then, once the therapist thoroughly understands each and every perspective, it becomes the job of the therapist to help you each see your partner's perspective and come to understand it as well as you understand your own. This important early stage of perspective sharing between each therapist-partner pair and the partner-partner pair is critical to the eventual successful outcome of therapy for you. So, please be patient as the relationship between you, your partner, and the therapist unfolds at the beginning stages. Research[1] has shown that what you bring to the table (your motivations, perspectives, and background) is 40% of whether or not therapy is successful and the therapist-patient relationship is another

3

KYLE N. WEIR, PHD, LMFT

30%. So, as you begin therapy in these early stages, fully 70% of the factors that will eventually affect the outcome are being addressed. That is why we are taking some considerable time to fully understand your issues and help build a good working therapeutic relationship between you, your partner, and your therapist.

Couples therapy works best when each partner is willing to look at their *own* contribution to problems in their relationship and avoid exclusively blaming all of the issues on their partner.[2] It takes two to tango. By focusing on what you have control over to change – namely, *yourself* (not your partner) – you can begin to become a powerful dynamo for change in the relationship. Therapy research has consistently[3] shown that changing one part of the system (in this case, yourself) can cause powerful ripple effects that change the whole family system.

Now, please focus on the problem or problems, issues, and concerns that brought the two of you in for couples therapy. In therapy terms we call this the *presenting problem*. In a few words (no more than a paragraph), each of you please describe your perception of the problem or problems that you would like to work on and resolve in couples therapy:

PARTNER 1:

PARTNER 2:

. . .

COLLABORATING FOR CONNECTION AS A COUPLE

IN YOUR NEXT session with your therapist, please be prepared to talk about your perception of the problem, including what you attribute the problem to or where you believe the problem stems from. In other words, what story or narrative do you tell yourself about why the problem keeps occurring in your relationship.

Also, please consider the following two questions: How have you and your partner tried in the past to team up against this problem? What has been the results of any efforts you have made to collaborate as a team against the problem?

Please answer the preceding questions jointly, if possible, after discussing your collaborative efforts (if any) have been attempted and describe why they were successful (or why they were not successful).

JOINT STATEMENT on Prior Team Efforts Against the Problem(s):

HOMEWORK – Chapter 1: Love Story

In addition to responding to the questions and prompts in this chapter, please reflect on the history of your relationship and be prepared to share your "love story" with your therapist. By love story, I mean: How did you meet? What were the circumstances? What first attracted you to each other? What obstacles did you have to overcome (if any) to come to be together? How has your relationship changed or stayed the same since your initial love story days?

KYLE N. WEIR, PHD, LMFT

Jot down notes about your love story you want to share with your therapist here:

_____
_____
_____
_____
_____
_____
_____
_____
_____
_____
_____
_____
_____
_____
_____

Recommended Readings

- John M. Gottman & Joan DeClaire (2001). *The Relationship Cure: A Five-Step Guide to Strengthening Your Marriage, Family, and Friendships.* New York, NY: Three Rivers Press.
- Paul Watzlawick, John H. Weakland, & Richard Fisch (1974; or 2011 Reprint Edition). *Change: Principles of Problem Formation and Problem Resolution.* New York, NY: W.W. Norton & Co.

CHAPTER TWO - COLLABORATION

Teamwork. The heart of a successful marriage or partnership is your ability to collaborate, or, in other words, work well as a team. There's been a lot of research about the principles of collaboration, particularly in the field of business studies and organizational theory. As a graduate student in the late 1990s, I first discovered the principles of conflict resolution as outlined by Drs. Kenneth W. Thomas and Ralph H. Kilmann in the 1970s while studying organizational theory and behavior. Over the decades, this model has been applied to numerous aspects of life such as resolving conflicts between agencies in a government system, business department squabbles, the development of pastors based on conflict management styles, bargaining and negotiation styles, and so much more. While I was learning about the Thomas-Kilmann Instrument (TKI)[1] I realized this model could easily be used with couples in couples therapy. So, I began using this model as a graduate student with the idea of promoting collaboration in couples' relationships. The results over the years have been astounding! This is why I came to believe that collaboration is the hallmark of a successful relationship. Couples who learn to collaborate well as a team weather the

7

KYLE N. WEIR, PHD, LMFT

storms and vicissitudes of life, and they also find they connect and feel closer to one another through their mutual efforts and history. Let's look at the model and learn how it can unleash powerful capacities in your relationship.

Figure 2
Conflict Resolution Styles

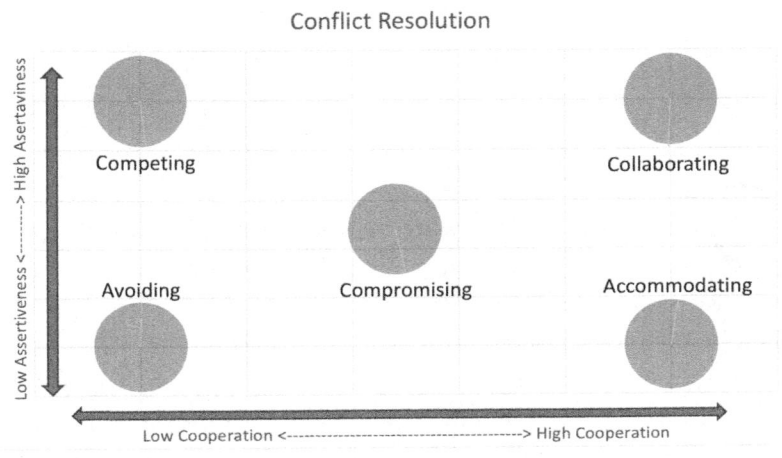

The basic idea behind this model of conflict resolution is that varying levels of assertiveness and cooperation lead to five basic conflict resolution styles. Let's define these terms:

- **Assertiveness** – A willingness and ability to express your needs, wants, and wishes. It is your voice. It is very different from aggressiveness, which is where violence, anger, and control exist. Assertiveness is often calm, but clear and firm. It usually begins with an "I-statement" such as "I need…" or "I want…" or "I hope…" without blaming the other person or partner. Generally speaking, needs are prioritized over wants and wishes when it comes to conflict resolution.

8

COLLABORATING FOR CONNECTION AS A COUPLE

- **Cooperation** – A willingness to work toward and meet your partner's needs, wants, and wishes. Cooperation is your efforts to help your partner get their needs met. Again, we tend to prioritize needs over wants and wishes, but the extent to which you cooperate to fulfill your partner's desires reflects greatly on the extent your collaboration abilities as a couple will develop.

- **Avoiding** – Low levels of assertiveness and low levels of cooperation. This one of the three "extreme styles" of conflict resolution that do NOT make for a satisfying marriage or relationship (the other two being competing and accommodating). Avoiding is a position one takes where they decide not to tell their partner what they need. Nor are they willing to help their partner with what their partner needs. Most couples do not start out avoiding each other. I've never known of anyone coming to their wedding altar with vows to *avoid* each other until "death do us part." Rather, most couples adopt an avoiding style over time. They have come to distrust that they can get their needs met by their partner through past experiences, so they have given up being assertive. They also resent not getting their needs met, so they withhold their cooperation. Throughout this CAST model we will see that trust and resentment play critical roles in the varying degrees of assertiveness and cooperation of partners.

- **Accommodating** – Low levels of assertiveness but high levels of cooperation. This conflict resolution style still exhibits the low levels of assertiveness (again usually because experience has taught them not to trust that their needs will get met), but they are still willing to cooperate at a high level. This may be because they are simply tired of the conflict and so they give in to keep the peace. Some people feel like a "door mat" and lack boundaries as they accommodate. Generally speaking, this accommodating mode of conflict does not last too long because resentment builds. When their resentment reaches a boiling point, they will likely shift to a competing style of conflict resolution because they drop their cooperation to a low level and increase their assertiveness.

- **Competing** – High levels of assertiveness and low levels of cooperation. This final style of the "extreme three" approaches is measured by the zero-sum nature through which the person views the world. For them life is a win/lose proposition. This competitive orientation may have come from a number of sources: learned behavior through sports, business, or other competitive ventures; a deep insecurity through not having their needs met throughout their life, or they may have been accommodating and just got fed up with that style, among many possible reasons. The competing style is the classic definition of selfishness, and selfishness doesn't usually make for good relationships.

- **Compromising** – Medium levels of assertiveness and cooperation denote the compromising style of conflict resolution. It is one of the two styles where relationships can function. Most couples have heard of a 50/50 style of marriage and assume compromising is the way to a happy marriage. It is not, however. A couple who compromises can function, but not thrive or flourish. The hallmark of the compromising style is its "count-keeping" nature. Most compromises are on a *quid pro quo* or "tit-for-tat" basis. A compromising couple is constantly calculating what it would cost them to get what they need. Like a political game in congress, there's a score-keeping nature, and the stakes are often high. Couples who adopt this approach can survive but there is usually some dissatisfaction in their relationship because they only get about half of their needs met and half-heartedly cooperate in meeting their partner's needs.

- **Collaborating** – High levels of assertiveness and high levels of cooperation simultaneously occurring. This is the "win/win" or "100/100" model of couples relationships. Collaboration involves the root words "co" and "labor" or working together. This team approach to marriage or other forms of coupling is the optimal form of a fulfilling relationship for both of them. It involves the coordinated effort of both partners having high levels of assertiveness and high levels of cooperation *at the same time.* When these collaborative experiences are repeated through consistent positive interactions, the couple begins to trust that their needs will be met and they are willing to work hard to meet their partner's needs. The collaborative couple does not engage in "count-keeping" or bargaining. Rather, they adopt the motto, "If it is important to you, it is important to us." They see themselves as a team and recognize both partners need to be fulfilled for the team to thrive, because you succeed or fail as a team, not as individuals. This isn't a zero-sum, win or lose scenario against each other. You are in it together. It can be difficult to consistently maintain the high ideal of collaboration, but collaborative couples strive for the ideal and readily course-correct when they are not functioning at the ideal collaborative level. Throughout these workbooks (and throughout the CAST model) collaboration is specifically defined as high assertiveness of one's own needs while simultaneously cooperating at high levels to meet one's partner's needs.

Take a moment to reflect on where you feel you are as an individual in these conflict resolution styles. What style is more comfortable for you personally? Through which style do you naturally tend to resolve conflict?

. . .

KYLE N. WEIR, PHD, LMFT

PARTNER 1:

_____

_____

_____

_____

_____

_____

_____

_____

_____

_____

PARTNER 2:

_____

_____

_____

_____

_____

_____

_____

_____

_____

WHICH STYLE DO you feel your partner tends to use and why do you feel that way?

PARTNER 1:

_____

_____

_____

Partner 2:

_____

_____

COLLABORATING FOR CONNECTION AS A COUPLE

IF YOU ARE WORKING with a trained CAST therapist or counselor, they should have had you take the Thomas-Kilmann Instrument (TKI) assessment test. Discuss with your therapist what scores you each received and record your conflict resolution style(s) here:

PARTNER 1:

PARTNER 2:

WHAT DO each of you feel needs to change (if any) so that your relationship can become a collaborative one?

PARTNER 1:

PARTNER 2:

KYLE N. WEIR, PHD, LMFT

. . .

MISMATCHED Conflict Resolution Styles Can Be Problematic, But CAST Helps Match Styles and Boost Emotional Attachment and Positivity

One credible researcher points out that mismatches in conflict resolutions styles and mismatches in how people process emotions tend to be more problematic for relationships[2] than most other factors of marital discontent. The significant benefit of Collaborative Attachment Systems Therapy (CAST) is that it helps couples match conflict resolution styles in the most productive and rewarding one possible – collaboration. By helping you and your partner team up collaboratively, you transform mismatched conflict management styles into a unified approach that is positive, supportive, and emotionally fulfilling.

As we proceed in these workbooks, you will see how this key task of collaborating helps increase trust, reduce resentment, increase positivity in your relationship, and build more secure attachments and closeness with one another. Unitedly collaborating as a loving partnership generates and unleashes many powerful attributes and tools in your marriage or relationship.

COLLABORATIVE PRINCIPLES CAN BE LEARNED and Applied

One of the beautiful things about this model that emphasizes collaboration is that the principles of collaboration can be taught, learned, and applied. Part of why the format of a workbook with a psycho-educational component at the beginning of each session was chosen for the CAST approach is that learning these collaborative principles is the first step to then later building a connected, attached, loving relationship. Throughout these workbooks, we will be exploring key collaborative principles that build successful loving couples relationships.

Many of these collaborative principles come from key researchers whose models are integrated together to form Collaborative Attach-

COLLABORATING FOR CONNECTION AS A COUPLE

ment Systems Therapy. Notable among the models integrated into CAST is the work of Dr. John Gottman from the University of Washington who has spent decades developing The Gottman Method (TGM)[3] of couples counseling by meticulously recording and observing thousands upon thousands of couples as he developed the principles outlined in his famous book *The Seven Principles for Making Marriage Work*.[4] Another key approach that is integrated into the CAST model is from the work of the late Dr. Carlfred B. Broderick, who was my mentor in graduate school at USC. Dr. Broderick was a masterful couples therapist, as well as a prolific researcher. Two of his books, *Couples: How to Confront Problems and Maintain Loving Relationships*,[5] and *Understanding Family Process: Basics of Family Systems Theory*,[6] are replete with important principles about collaboration, cooperation, dealing with resentment, and many other learnable tenets of successful relationships. Dr. William Doherty's book *Take Back Your Marriage*[7] is also influential in CAST. He is a professor, marriage and family therapist, and family scholar from the University of Minnesota – Twin Cities.

Once the collaborative principles from Gottman, Broderick, Doherty and others have been learned, the work of Dr. Sue Johnson and others on attachment theory will be applied in an experiential manner. That means the middle phases of CAST involve applying what you have learned in your relationship experiences at home and in therapy sessions. In the later phases of CAST you will also be learning and applying several collaborative principles along the TRAIL to Love by focusing on 12 "Collaborative Tasks for Couples" that will enrich your relationship, help you overcome obstacles and challenges, and aid you as you work together for the loving relationship you both desire.

HOMEWORK – **Chapter 2: Collaboration Discussion**

This week please identify for yourself three things you can be more assertive about and three things you could be more cooperative about in your relationship. Go on a date and have a discussion where

15

KYLE N. WEIR, PHD, LMFT

you each express 2-3 needs to your partner and plan how you can be more collaborative with each other.

PARTNER 1: Assertive

PARTNER 1: Cooperative

PARTNER 2: Assertive

PARTNER 2: Cooperative

RECOMMENDED READINGS*

- Carlfred B. Broderick (1979). *Couples: How to Confront Problems and Maintain Loving Relationships.* New York, NY: Simon & Schuster, Inc.
- John M. Gottman & Nan Silver (2015). The *Seven Principles*

for Making Marriage Work. New York, NY: Three Rivers Press.

*I HIGHLY RECOMMEND both of these books as much of the CAST approach is built on the works of John Gottman and Carlfred Broderick, as well as Bill Doherty and Sue Johnson (who we will learn about in future chapters).

CHAPTER THREE - ATTACHMENT: THEORY

*W*hat are the differences in parenting styles between mother sea turtles and human beings? A mother sea turtle crawls onto land, digs a large hole into the sand, lays hundreds of eggs, buries the eggs in the sand, and returns to sea. That's it. That is her sole parenting responsibility. The hatchlings are left to fend for themselves. They hatch from their shell, climb onto the beach and race for the ocean. Small mammals, crabs, and other predators feast upon them while they are on land. Once the sea turtles reach the ocean, birds and fish are waiting to consume them. Estimates on how many baby sea turtles grow to full maturity range from 1 out of 1,000 to 1 out of 10,000.[1]

The parenting role of humans is much different. Most human mothers produce one child per pregnancy, but occasionally there are twins, triplets or other multiple children per birth – certainly not hundreds like the sea turtles. The baby or babies are born, not hatched, and are not capable of walking, crawling, or surviving on their own initially like the sea turtle hatchlings. If a mother were to leave her newborn infant in the wilderness to fend for itself, like the mama sea turtle does, the human infant would almost certainly not survive. But statistically, the current youth mortality rate (the

COLLABORATING FOR CONNECTION AS A COUPLE

percentage of children who die before age 15 years) is at 4.6% globally.[2] So, given the statistical facts, why do sea turtles have at best 1 in a 1,000 chance of reaching maturity and humans have a 954 in a 1,000 chance of reaching the age where they could reproduce? Bonding. Bonding is the answer. Human beings, like most mammals, are biologically inspired to care for their young until they reach maturity.

Interestingly, bonding is a biological response to procreating that most humans feel for their children. But the biological nature of bonding is typically a one-way street. Parents bond to their children, but children don't necessarily bond to parents. Instead there is a related, but slightly different element at play that causes a two-way connection between parents and a child. That form of connection is called *attachment*.

Attachment is a two-way street, so to speak, that is based on social experiences. Attachment is a *socially learned* response instead of a biological one (this point becomes very important to your marriage or relationship in just a moment). Imagine there is a newborn infant in a crib. The child experiences some discomfort in his or her stomach area. The child has no verbal skills. Developmentally, they cannot speak, "I'm hungry" yet. So, what does the baby do? The baby cries. That's his or her job. Hopefully, what does the mother do? She comes and feeds her baby. From the baby's perspective the mother is some "object" or being that makes the yucky feeling of hunger go away. When the pattern of getting his or her needs met occurs *consistently* in a loving, nurturing way, the baby begins to emotionally attach to this "thing-that-feeds-me" which he or she later learns to call "mama." A similar experience occurs with the father. If the baby feels a yucky sensation because it has peed or pooped himself or herself, the baby does its job by crying. If the father, or someone else, consistently comes and makes that yucky feeling go away by changing the baby's diaper, the baby starts to attach to the other nurturing caretaker in his or her life.

Fortunately, this pattern of attachment can happen with multiple people. If the baby is bored and big brother or sister makes faces or plays kindly with the baby, the infant-sibling attachment begins to

19

form. Attachments occur in multiple directions in multiple relationships based on the social interactions the infant has with the caregivers and other family that surrounds and supports him or her. What builds healthy attachments are consistent, reliable, and positive social interactions where the baby feels cared for, loved, valued, safe, and secure. *Consistency of positive social interactions is the key to building healthy attachments.*

The same is also true for marital and other romantic relationships. Romantic relationships that predictably and consistently experience positive interactions between the partners that conveys love, care, support, trust, commitment, safety, security, connection, and value build healthy attachments in those relationships. Thankfully, attachment is sociological, not biological. We do not have to be genetically related to our romantic partners to build attachment to them (in fact, it would be quite awkward to do so with our genetic relatives). The sociological nature of attachment allows for foster and adoptive families to attach despite not being genetically related to one another. This same benefit of social-experiential based forms of attachment, as opposed to the biologically based bonding process, is what allows romantic couples to attach, as well. And a key correlate to that notion is that whatever is socially created can be socially changed. There is not a biological block or impediment to changing attachment patterns from unhealthy to healthy. Because the attachment patterns of your romantic relationship have been socially constructed through experiences (for good or bad), those attachment patterns can be socially healed and changed through new patterns of positive interactions that you will learn in these workbooks and apply at home and in therapy sessions. That's why it is so important to distinguish the biological bonding from socially derived attachment.

In the latter part of the 20th century Dr. John Bowlby – a British psychiatrist at the Tavistock Clinic in London – began studying the attachment patterns of mother-child relationships. A student of Bowlby, Dr. Mary Ainsworth of the University of Virginia, began classifying styles of attachment. She indicated three styles of attachment:

COLLABORATING FOR CONNECTION AS A COUPLE

- **Secure Attachment** – the child perceives the parent(s) as safe, secure, and valuing of them because the parents consistently meet the child's needs in a loving, nurturing manner.
- **Anxious/Ambivalent** – the child anxiously wants to be loved by the parents, but often feels ambivalent when love is shown to them. This is because the parents are *inconsistent*[3] * and the child never knows if the caring parent or the harsh parent is going to show up. The inconsistency makes the child distrustful of the positive care they sometimes receive.
- **Avoidant** – the parents who form this style of attachment are consistent – just consistently bad. The parents are hurtful, disappointing, dismissive, neglectful, or abusive on a regular basis. The child learns to avoid human relationships because they have learned that relationships just end up hurting them. So, the child ends up behaving in ways to push people away, protect themselves, and try to "go it alone" in a counterfeit of self-reliance (often to the point of feeling lonely, but too defiant to admit it).

DR. SUE JOHNSON *and Adult Romantic Attachments*

Dr. Sue Johnson, Emeritus Professor of Psychology at the University of Ottowa, along with her mentor Dr. Les Greenberg, developed a model of couples therapy called Emotionally Focused Therapy (EFT). Her brilliant idea was to examine how adult romantic attachments are similar to the developmental parent-child attachments Dr. John Bowlby studied. Years of research by Dr. Johnson and her colleagues have demonstrated a clear connection between romantic partnerships and attachment patterns. Her work revolutionized couples therapy approaches and provided empirical validation of the effectiveness of her form of couples therapy. Similar to John Gottman's TGM model

KYLE N. WEIR, PHD, LMFT

of couples therapy, Sue Johnson's EFT has success rates between 70-75%[4] and is a valuable model in and of itself. CAST builds on the work of Sue Johnson, John Gottman, Carlfred Broderick, and others by integrating the principles of collaboration and attachment they teach and then applying them in an informative and experiential way to build a better collaborative attachment in your relationship.

The Emotionally Focused Therapy (EFT) model is introduced to the general audience in a wonderful book that I highly recommend called *Hold Me Tight: Seven Conversations for a Lifetime of Love.*[5] In a reader-friendly version of EFT, Dr. Johnson leads you on a journey of understanding about love and attachment that will help you recognize and overcome "Demon Dialogues," "Raw Spots," "Rocky Moments," and many other obstacles that prevent you from attaching in what she calls "Hold Me Tight" relationships. Whether your relational "dancing" style is "Find the Bad Guy," the "Protest Polka," or "Freeze and Flee," her book can help you understand how your patterns of interaction create a cycle that subverts your desire and capacity to connect and fulfill each other's needs. She also has ingenious solutions to help you team up against that cycle and learn to soften your hearts toward one another as you build new relational styles of interaction.

Sue Johnson's Emotionally Focused Therapy (EFT) involves nine steps in three basic stages.[6] The first stage involves cycle de-escalation and includes steps 1-4. The first step is to identify the relational conflict between the both of you. Then identify the underlying interaction cycle (which is often referred to through EFT as "the cycle") where the problematic issues are manifest. Third, access the unacknowledged emotions underlying the interactional position each partner takes in this cycle. Fourth, reframe the problem in terms of the cycle, accompanying underlying emotions, and attachment needs. The goal of this first stage (steps 1-4) is to help you, the couple, develop a more objective perspective about how your interactions are unwittingly created by your cycle, validate each of your perspectives, come together as a couple against your common enemy (the cycle), and begin to initiate a cycle that builds a happier and more fulfilling attachment connection in your relationship.

COLLABORATING FOR CONNECTION AS A COUPLE

The second stage of EFT is about changing your interactional positions. This stage includes steps 5-7. Step five is about helping you identify with your own disowned attachment emotions, needs, and aspects of self. Step six is concerned with promoting acceptance by each partner of the other partner's experience. Step seven involves facilitating the expression of needs and wants to restructure the interaction based on the new understandings and create bonding events. The main goals of this stage are to have the partners who are withdrawn from one another learn to re-engage one another, have couples who are accusatory and blaming learn to "soften" towards one another, and have all couples ask for their attachment needs from a vulnerable position. The theory rests on these softening experiences where you become more accessible, responsive, and engaged.

The final stage involves consolidation and integration and includes steps 8 and 9. Step eight is where the therapist helps the couple to find new solutions to old problems. Step nine involves consolidating your new interactional positions and healthier cycles of attachment. The main goals in this concluding stage are to summarize, support, and solidify the progress you have made.

Your CAST therapist will be using elements of EFT in their work, but will likely do things in a slightly different order or manner because CAST integrates many, many models of therapy into one. But it is important for you to see these steps as general guidelines for how we hope to change your relationship in a way that will bring about healthier attachments and more connected emotions between the two of you.

TAKE a few moments and reflect on your childhood years. Based on what you have learned about attachment in this chapter, how would you characterize you attachment patterns with your parents, caretakers, or other significant family members during your growing up years?

·   ·   ·

23

KYLE N. WEIR, PHD, LMFT

PARTNER 1:

_____

_____

_____

PARTNER 2:

_____

_____

_____

IN WHAT WAYS do you see your early attachment needs and styles affecting your current romantic relationship?

PARTNER 1:

_____

_____

_____

PARTNER 2:

_____

_____

_____

WHAT ARE some of the deep feelings and attachment needs each of you would like to bring up with your partner and therapist in the next session?

Partner 1:

_____

_____

_____

PARTNER 2:

_____

_____

_____

LOVE, *Trust, and Commitment's Critical Role in Attachment*

In the early part of my career, I spent considerable time researching about and providing therapy for foster and adoptive families. I wrote extensively about research I conducted about play therapy with foster and adoptive families, I worked as a foster family agency social worker in Pasadena, CA, and I still engage in expert witnessing for the courts about attachment matters for foster and adoptive families. I learned there are a few critical things every foster and/or adopted child needs. They need the consistency and commitment that comes from having a permanent plan for family. They need to know their new parents are committed to them through thick and thin, no matter what. They need to be able to trust their new parents and family members through hard experiences. Lastly, they need love, though they may resist that at first. Permanent commitment, transparent trust, and unconditional love are essential for the foster or adopted child to develop a healthy attachment with their new parents and family.

Much like consistency, permanency, care, and trustworthiness are essential for building healthy, secure attachments in the parent-child relationship, the attributes of consistency, commitment, care, love, and trustworthiness are essential for successful romantic relationship attachments. In fact, several models of therapy emphasize trust and commitment as part of their approaches. Dr. Ivan Boszormenyi-Nagy, the founder of Contextual Family Therapy, famously said:

"The essence of therapy and of any human relationship is a capacity for commitment and trust."[7]

Take a moment and reflect on your level commitment to your relationship. Are you all in? Not sure or ambivalent? If you have some hesitancy to fully committing to your relationship, can you identify what barriers (for example, lack of trust, lack of feeling connected or attached, not feeling valued, among others)? Rather than writing them down now, please prepare to discuss these concerns you may have (if any) with your therapist during your next couples therapy session.

HOMEWORK – Chapter 3: Practicing Softening

Taking into account the attachment patterns from your family or origin while you were growing up and the attachment patterns of your partner in his or her upbringing, have a conversation with your partner about how your childhood attachment patterns may be affecting your romantic attachment patterns in your relationship. Be sure to emphasize understanding and empathizing rather than judging or fixing. Try to listen and be soft and kind to your partner while you talk about the attachment patterns from your past. Avoid blaming or accusing in your present relationship. Just try to work together in order to lovingly understand how childhood attachment patterns may be influencing your relationship now. Most important in this homework is how you respond to your partner. The key is to have softer, kindlier responses to one another while talking about potentially vulnerable, sensitive experiences and feelings.

If this seems too difficult to do face to face, try completing this assignment by writing letters. Or, alternatively, this would be an ideal conversation to have in a therapy session with your CAST trained therapist if you aren't sure how to go about having such a conversation on your own.

Recommended Readings

- Sue Johnson (2008). *Hold Me Tight: Seven Conversations for a Lifetime of Love.* New York, NY: Little, Brown and Company.

CHAPTER FOUR - SYSTEMS AS A WAY TO REBUILD RELATIONSHIPS

*D*o you ever notice that the pattern of your arguments seems to go around and around – often about the same things – like watching an old re-run on TV that you've seen many times before? That's because of something marriage and family therapists call "systems theory." It is the core belief system that makes marriage and family therapists different from psychologists, social workers, and other types of mental health providers. Good family therapists are always looking below the surface content of your arguments to see the deeper, underlying patterns of your relationship. There are some basic principles therapists have noticed about relationships:

- Circular Causality – Relationship patterns usually don't have a start and a finish. Rather they tend to result from spiraling interactions that feedback and influence one another like a chain reaction. For example, a husband may initiate sexual intimacy. The wife may decline. The husband, fearing that his wife isn't attracted to him as much anymore, may try harder to get her to be physically intimate with him. His wife, fearing her husband won't take no for an answer, declines and distances herself even more.

27

Because she distances, he pursues her even harder. Because he pursues her harder, she increases her distancing more forcefully. The pattern goes around and around each person increasing their "solution" to the problem that only increases the problem and polarizes their positions further and further apart. In effect, their "solution" to the problem IS the problem, and the couple is engaging in a classic pattern called a "pursuer-distancer" relationship.

- Triangles – When people are anxious or don't know how to deal directly with each other, they often pull a third party into the relationship system. Perhaps in high school, you romantically liked someone but were too nervous to tell them directly so you chose to tell a mutual friend to see if they would find out if the other person liked you back. Many movies and literature have plots that feature such love triangles. In your relationship, the things you triangulate into your relationship may be concerns about your children, dealing with in-laws or friends, technology such as smart phones and tablets that seem to get in between the two of you. All of these and more can be examples of unhealthy triangles. Triangles sometimes have the advantage of decreasing anxiety and stabilizing tense situations, but they are usually considered harmful to your relationship to the extent that they freeze your conflicts in place so you can't make progress and they cause emotional disconnect and detachment.

- Balance or "Homeostasis" – The more things change, the more they stay the same. You try to make changes and improvements in your relationship, but it feels like you are just "spinning your wheels" so to speak. You make an effort to improve things and it seems like that is the moment that your partner does more of what annoys you the most. For every move you make, it seems like there is a countermove occurring somewhere in your family relationships – either your spouse's behaviors, your children's needs, or work

COLLABORATING FOR CONNECTION AS A COUPLE

demands always seem to get in the way of your efforts to be closer and happier in your family relationships. That's because systems, such as family systems, like to stay in balance. There is a certain amount of equilibrium or what therapists call "homeostasis" that seems to offset changes and keep things the way they are. Many people are uncomfortable with change – even good changes – so they would rather stay with what they know that is stable than have unknown changes that may or may not make things better. Homeostasis is a natural resistance to change. Therapists often have to predict the homeostatic patterns that fight change so the families will know what to expect and how to overcome the balance-counterbalance obstacles.

- Communication and Meta-Communication Patterns – Communication in family systems involves at least a sender and receiver, the medium of communication, the message, and the meta-message. It can get more complex from there, but therapists will be examining how you and your partner communicate, how you communicate (in-person, phone, text, etc.), what you say, and how you say it. Meta-Communication is essentially stepping back from the communication patterns to see the rules of communication, the role people play, and the meta-messages (the tone, gestures, and inflections) that define the messages of communication and ultimately define the relational interactions. Everything you say or do (or don't say or do) is communication in one way or another. One of the earliest family therapy researchers, Paul Watzlawick and his colleagues, famously stated: "one cannot *not* communicate."[1] Even if a client or patient sits silently and stares out the window refusing to talk to the therapist or their partner, that speaks volumes about how they feel about therapy in that moment.

- Non-summativity – Family systems are more than just summing up the individual parts. Each family seems to have an interactive or synergistic effect in their relationships when they are together. As therapists, we can't just look at the individual people to explain all that goes on in a family system. There is something about putting all of the people of a family together that makes clearer the whole picture of what is going on. That's why therapists often want to bring more than one person (often many people) into counseling sessions. While changing one part of the family system can have a ripple effect on the whole system, research has shown that healing often occurs significantly better, significantly faster when working in a couple or family context.[2]

- Structure, Hierarchy, and Leadership – All families have certain rhythms. The patterned ways a family does things is what therapists call "structure." Family structure provides the rules around which a family can organize itself. For example, on cold winter mornings, I often get up and start a fire in our wood burning stove to warm the house up while my wife makes breakfast for the family before the kids go to school. It doesn't have to be that way. She could start the fire and I could cook but I'm better at starting a fire and she is a far better cook than I am. We don't have to ask each other each day who wants to do what. We just get up and do the same things we've done in the past because that pattern has worked best for our family over time. Our winter mornings have naturally taken on that structure over the years which allows each of us to organize or know how to act in our roles. Roles don't have to be rigid or prescribed by certain traits like gender or age, but every family has a way for determining the structured pattern of how they operate in life. One key element that flows from structure is, "Who's in charge?" Roles in structured family patterns do tend to take on a hierarchy. Again, these don't have to be rigid, but it is necessary that someone provides leadership to the family. Hopefully, as a couple, you work together to

COLLABORATING FOR CONNECTION AS A COUPLE

collaboratively provide leadership to your family and children (if you have any). Research has shown family structure works best when the adults are in charge of the children in a nurturing context[3] and not the other way around. If children are "running the roost" so to speak, the leadership by the adults is lacking and needs to be re-balanced with the help of a therapist.

THESE ARE JUST a few of the basic premises therapists consider when working with a new family. Though it may be that only the two of you, as a couple, attend therapy sessions, the therapist should consider your couple's relationship as a subsystem of a larger family system and may look to see where other influences (for example, your children, in-laws, work colleagues and career demands, friendships, and other relationships in your community) impact in either a beneficial or harmful way to your marriage or relationship.

SYSTEMICALLY JUMP STARTING A "REPAIR ATTEMPT" by Collaborating, Increasing Trust, and Reducing Resentment: The Collaboration-Trust-Resentment (CTR) Cycle

At all points in the CAST model along the TRAIL to Love, systems processes are in effect. Systems theory permeates all throughout your family's life, so it also permeates all throughout this therapy approach. But there is one particular way that systems theory is evident in your relationship that the CAST approach highlights. That is how the concepts of *trust* and *resentment* play significant roles in either helping or deterring you from being able to collaborate in your relationship (and how collaboration can also increase trust and reduce resentment).

Remember that our goal of *collaboration* was defined as simulta-neous high levels of assertiveness and high levels of cooperation. So, examining factors that impact assertiveness and cooperation are key

31

KYLE N. WEIR, PHD, LMFT

to enabling collaboration. I will use graphs I developed based on the Thomas-Kilmann modes of conflict resolution to highlight these systemic processes.

It seems clear that in order to have high assertiveness at least one of the partners must trust that they might get their needs met if they are assertive. So, based on that variable modicum of "one-sided" trust (meaning they trust enough to assert, but not cooperate), they will assert themselves. But often people will have some resentment over past times when they did not get their needs met so they may not be as willing to cooperate in meeting their partner's needs (their high resentment overrides their cooperation). For arguing couples, this common stance (high assertiveness, low cooperation) is called *competing* in the Thomas-Kilmann mode and may look something like this:

Figure 3

A Competing Partner's Levels of Trust and Resentment

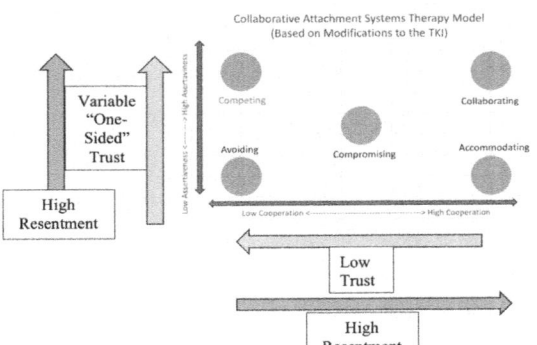

Figure 3
A Competing Partner's Levels of Trust and Resentment

COLLABORATING FOR CONNECTION AS A COUPLE

IF YOU ARE COMPETING with your partner, the fact that you are arguing demonstrates that you have at least some level of trust that you can get your needs met if you "win" the argument (even if that amount of trust is small). You wouldn't argue if you had *zero* hope. Your arguing (though perhaps done in a way that is misguided and counterproductive) is an assertive expression that you might convince your partner to meet your needs if you can "just get through" to them. Arguing shows that you trust just enough to assert, but don't trust enough to cooperate. I call this "variable" or "one-sided" trust because it is trust in only one aspect – assertiveness, but low trust in cooperation. Arguing and competing is most likely NOT the best way of getting your partner to cooperate in meeting your needs, because you are not cooperating in return. CAST teaches you there are better ways of being assertive and cooperative that will more likely accomplish your goals if you approach your partner in a more loving, collaborative way than competing.

To get the couple system moving in the right direction, it often takes at least one spouse to show leadership and take an initial "leap of faith" – faith in their partner, faith in the relationship, and/or faith in your future together. The leading spouse needs to drop their resentment and demonstrate high trust in both dimensions by simultaneously being assertive AND cooperative. Being assertive and cooperative at the same time can be hard to do, but increasing your trust in both being highly assertive and being highly cooperative should start a systemic spiral or chain reaction. (Remember the concept of circular causality mentioned earlier in this chapter? This is where it is applied.) This act of faith typically starts with what Dr. John Gottman calls a "***repair attempt***."[4]

KYLE N. WEIR, PHD, LMFT

Figure 4

Leading Spouse (Starts with Trust): "Act of Faith: Repair Attempt"

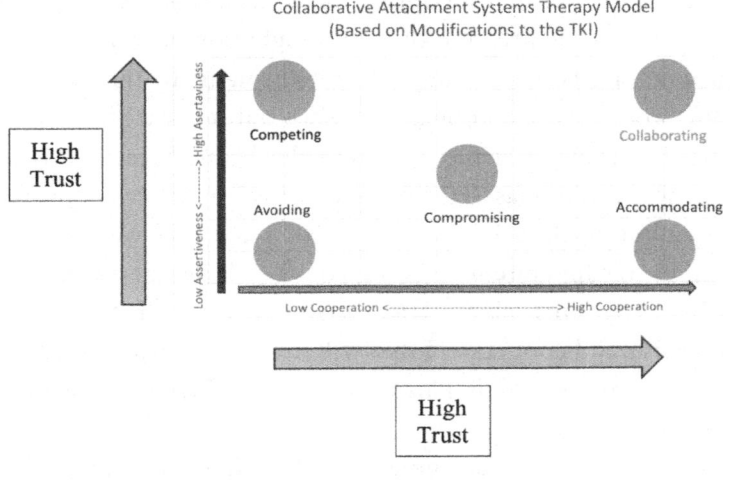

Y<small>OUR</small> <small>REPAIR</small> <small>ATTEMPT</small> will usually begin as you soften your voice and your heart to your partner. Most couples have a way of preventing the conflict from escalating. A repair attempt could be a heartfelt, "I'm sorry" or a silly face that breaks the tension. It could be anything that works for the two of you. The key is to find some actions, phrases, or gestures that communicates with your partner that you are trying to reach out to them, having faith in them and/or your relationship, increasing your trust by being cooperative along with your assertiveness, and signaling your desire to collaborate as a teammate with them.

You possess trust that by cooperating in meeting your partner's needs while also being assertive of your own needs, you will be able to help your partner reduce their resentment and begin to build trust in you. The goal is that the spouse who responds to the other's gentle leadership will soften their responses and reduce resentment.

COLLABORATING FOR CONNECTION AS A COUPLE

Figure 5

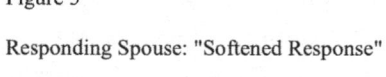

Responding Spouse: "Softened Response"

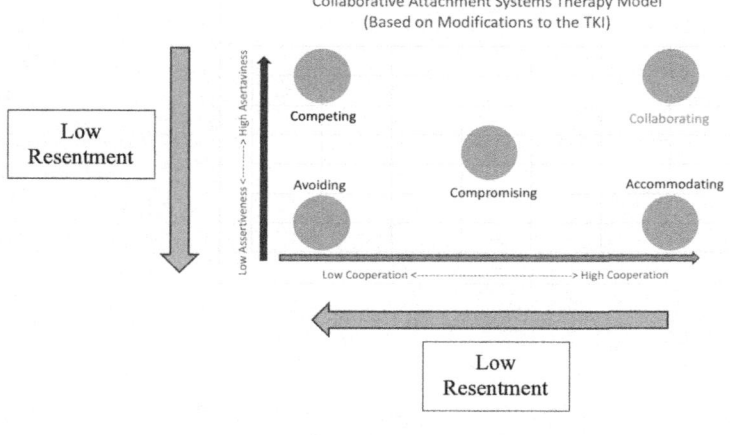

WHETHER YOU ARE the leading spouse or the responding spouse, the key is that by focusing on collaboration you can increase your trust and reduce resentment to jump start a relational turnaround cycle that builds positive interactions, even better collaboration, and deeper attachment connections with one another. Once the cycle begins to take root in your relationship, you will start to have repeating cycles of more collaborative actions, increasing levels of trust, and decreasing resentment. These repeating cycles will feel like positive interactions that spiral in the desired direction. I call these cycles **Collaboration-Trust-Resentment or CTR** cycles because the core ingredients we need to monitor in your interactions are collaboration (or lack of collaboration, as measured by levels of assertiveness and levels of cooperation determining which other conflict resolution styles you and your partner are employing), your level of trust, and your level of resentment. Once the repeating cycles start moving in the right direc-

35

KYLE N. WEIR, PHD, LMFT

tion, your *consistent* collaboration will build a better attachment and love between you and your spouse or partner. I call this **converting the cycle** because you are changing or converting what used to be a negative cycle within you and between you into a repeating positive cycle. An internal positive CTR cycle process will look something like this repeating over and over:

Figure 6

Positive Reflexive Spiraling Cycle: "Collaboration-Trust-Resentment" (CTR) Cycle

Collaborative Attachment Systems Therapy Model
(Based on Modifications to the TKI)

Competing

Collaborating

Avoiding

Compromising

Accommodating

High Assertiveness

Low Assertiveness

Low Cooperation ←--------------------→ High Cooperation

Increasing Trust

Decreasing Resentment

Increasing Trust

Decreasing Resentment

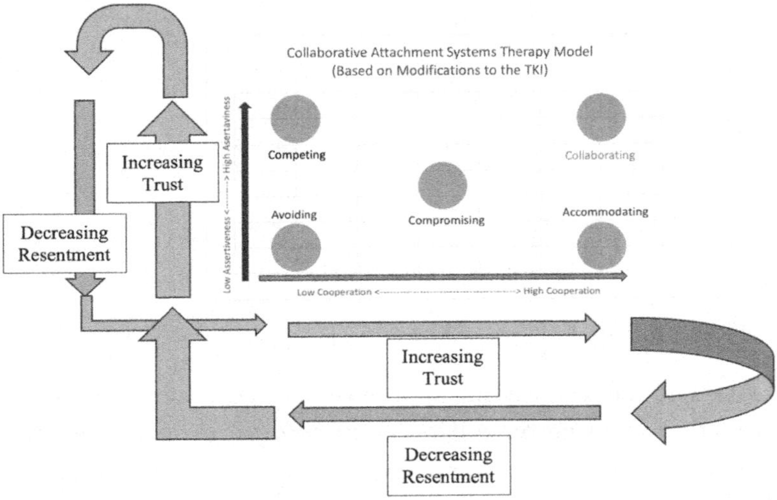

NOTICE that the high levels of trust and low levels of resentment boost both assertiveness and cooperation to high levels (i.e. collaboration). The collaboration style that the first partner generates and then reciprocally experiences back will then aid the second partner to experience lower levels of resentment, higher levels of trust, and a desire to collaborate with their partner. As both partners experience a positive Collaboration-Trust-Resentment (CTR) cycle *within* themselves, they will desire to have that same positive CTR cycle *between* themselves in their relationship. I notate that with the following expression:

36

COLLABORATING FOR CONNECTION AS A COUPLE

Figure 7

Positive Interpersonal Collaboration-Trust-Resentment Cycle Between Both Partners

Partner 1   Partner 2

$$\text{CTR} + \infty \ \text{CTR} +$$

This illustrates that partner 1 has achieved a positive CTR cycle where they have high trust, low resentment, and an approach toward their partner that is collaborative. If partner 2 is also experiencing a positive CTR cycle, this process becomes a wellspring of positivity that is expressed and reciprocated repeatedly (hence the infinity symbol between the partners).

As you well know, couples do not always have positive feelings about each other or themselves. They also don't have the Collaboration-Trust-Resentment cycle working in the right direction. This is where the research of Dr. John Gottman helps us. In his book *The Science of Trust,*[5] Gottman uses an academic technique called "game theory" to develop a matrix of possible interactions based on if partners are nice, neutral, or nasty toward one another. Though many possible combinations exist, we will focus on just three of them: Nice-Nice, Neutral-Neutral, and Nasty-Nasty. I would theorize that when one partner is experiencing a positive CTR cycle within themselves it leads them to be "nice" toward their partner. Their partner may or may not respond in kind. The conflict resolution style of compromising would lead to a "neutral" interaction approach and a neutral CTR cycle because the partner has medium levels of trust, some lingering but not overwhelming resentment and is willing to work with their partner to a degree as long as the count-keeping balance seems somewhat fair. When a partner employs one of the "extreme three" forms of conflict resolution (competing, accommodating, or avoiding) the interaction approach could be classified as "nasty" because there is either low trust, high resentment, or both leading to

37

KYLE N. WEIR, PHD, LMFT

low levels of assertiveness and/or cooperation. As we will see in a subsequent chapter, the key finding from Gottman's research is to reduce the amount of time spent in the Nasty-Nasty interactions. One way a couple can do this is to focus on converting their cycle from a negative CTR cycle to at least a neutral or (preferably) positive CTR cycle. Thus, we would try to convert the following cycle from this:

Figure 8

CTR Cycles with Key Conversion Combination Possibilities

Partner 1 Partner 2

(Nasty) CTR – ∞ CTR – (Nasty)

To either this:

Partner 1 Partner 2

(Neutral) CTR ~ ∞ CTR ~ (Neutral)

Or this:

Partner 1 | Partner 2

(Nice) CTR + ∞ CTR + (Nice)*

---

* For most of the workbook I will use the following notation form to represent all the possible combinations of CTR cycles and their corresponding Nice, Neutral, or Nasty interactions:

CTR ⋮ ∞ CTR ⋮

38

COLLABORATING FOR CONNECTION AS A COUPLE

As INDIVIDUALS AND AS A COUPLE, you can use the initials CTR from the Collaboration-Trust-Resentment cycle as a reminder to "choose the right" cycle. In other words, you can think of the acronym CTR and think about whether you want to choose a positive, neutral, or negative cycle by either being "nice" by collaborating," "neutral" by compromising, or "nasty" by competing, accommodating, or avoiding, knowing that levels of trust and resentment will correspond to your decisions. The choice in every interaction is yours.

While the whole process may seem complex, it can essentially be simple. When one spouse or partner takes an act of faith in the relationship by engaging a repair attempt, their trust ensures that they are interacting with high cooperation with their partner's needs while simultaneously maintaining high assertiveness of their own needs. Trust in collaboration is the key to activating gestures of repair and positive CTR cycles. Hopefully, the responding spouse or partner will recognize their counterpart's repair attempt and respond with a softened, less resentful response. Then, ideally, the responding spouse or partner increases their trust and offers a repair attempt of their own signaling to the leading spouse that they, in turn, are willing to collaborate by being highly cooperative and assertive. As the couple experiences these positive CTR cycles of collaboration through these powerfully escalating trust levels and corresponding reduced resentment levels repeatedly, they will develop a deeper attachment to one another.

This systemic process can increase collaboration and attachment in your marriage or partnership. It starts with increasing trust, which is why trust is the first step in the TRAIL to Love. Learning about trust – what trust is, how to increase it, what barriers may exist to building trust, or how to rebuild it if it has been lost by serious violations of expectations, standards, or values – is essential if your marital or partnered cycle-system will be able to be converted to the positive CTR cycle described above. Workbook 2 will further address the critical element of trust in relationships in greater detail, but please

39

KYLE N. WEIR, PHD, LMFT

reflect on where you think the level of trust is between the two of you in your relationship.

PARTNER 1:

_____

_____

_____

PARTNER 2:

_____

_____

_____

WHAT IS one concrete thing you can do to be more trustworthy to your partner?

PARTNER 1:

_____

_____

_____

PARTNER 2:

_____

_____

_____

WHICH SYSTEMIC CONCEPTS from this chapter would you like more information about or would like to ask your CAST trained therapist about?

COLLABORATING FOR CONNECTION AS A COUPLE

. . .

PARTNER 1:

_____

_____

_____

PARTNER 2:

_____

_____

_____

WHAT PATTERN or cycle do you feel stuck in? What problems just keep happening over and over?

PARTNER 1:

_____

_____

_____

PARTNER 2:

_____

_____

_____

HOW CAN YOU "CHOOSE THE RIGHT" Collaboration-Trust-Resentment cycle (CTR +, ~, or −) to help your interactions as a couple move from wherever they currently are along the Nasty-Neutral-Nice spectrum to more Nice-Nice interactions?

. . .

41

KYLE N. WEIR, PHD, LMFT

PARTNER 1:

_____

_____

_____

PARTNER 2:

_____

_____

_____

LASTLY, think about any phrases, actions, or gestures that you could use as a repair attempt. What has worked in the past? What new repair attempt would you like to try. Write them down.

PARTNER 1:

_____

_____

_____

PARTNER 2:

_____

_____

_____

HOMEWORK – **Chapter 4: System Repairs**

Each of you identify one thing in your relationship that you would like to change or repair. It doesn't have to be a big problem, in fact this will probably work better if you practice on a small problem first. Have a conversation about how each of your "solutions to the problem" sometimes makes the problem worse. Be sure to examine your

COLLABORATING FOR CONNECTION AS A COUPLE

own role and not blame your partner. Talk about how you can be more cooperative with your partner around that issue while still being assertive about any key needs you may have concerning the issue. Then practice trying to trust. Trust yourself by trying to be more cooperative and assertive. Try trusting your partner and giving him or her the benefit of the doubt.

After having the conversation about this issue, plan to do something together that has nothing to do with the issue. Maybe go out on a date or do some fun activity together. Focus on trying to increase positive interactions with one another. See if you can jump start positive cycles in your relationship. Throughout the following days, if a moment of tension or anger surfaces, try some type of repair attempt that you wrote down in this chapter. Test to see if your repair attempts can change the systemic cycles in your relationship.

RECOMMENDED Readings

- Shelly Smith-Acuña (2010). *Systems Theory in Action: Applications to Individual, Couple, and Family Therapy.* Hoboken, NJ: John Wiley & Sons.

CHAPTER FIVE - THERAPY: A PLANNED INTERLUDE TO ADDRESS YOUR ISSUES AND CHALLENGES IN THE CONTEXT OF CAST

*L*et's take a moment– an interlude or planned paused break – before we commence on the TRAIL to Love to ensure that you, your partner, and your therapist are addressing your issues and challenges in the context of the Collaborative Attachment Systems Therapy (CAST) model. After all, therapy is not a "one-size-fits-all" process. Additionally, we recognize that people come from different cultural, religious, ethnic, socio-economic, sexual orientation, and other diverse backgrounds. Therapy must be conducted and/or modified in a culturally sensitive way to these diversity factors.

There may be particular issues or challenges that you and your partner need to bring up at this point in the process of therapy. Take a moment to write down 2-3 things that you would like to address in therapy that may be unique to your situation.

PARTNER 1:

COLLABORATING FOR CONNECTION AS A COUPLE

. . .

PARTNER 2:

_____

_____

_____

THERAPY CAN BE REALLY CHALLENGING. In a class lesson, Dr. Carlfred Broderick once compared therapy to surgery. Just as a surgeon cuts into a patient, explores the problem or pathology from the inside and outside perspectives, has to remove certain problematic parts, may have to replace those areas with new parts, and warns that the patient may actually feel more short-term pain because of the surgery but will ultimately be healthier in the long-term, therapy can feel like a similar process. Therapist have to dig deep into feelings and perspectives that may be uncomfortable to review or relive. There will likely be problematic behaviors and thoughts that will need to be altered, reframed, or removed altogether. Accepting some short-term pain through the therapy process because you are aware of the long-term healthier benefits that follow can be difficult. But in the end, most people feel it was worth it and that their relationship improved. But in the early stages, some couples wonder if therapy is making things better or worse.

I often compare the process of therapy to cleaning out a messy closet. No one really looks forward to the task, but we all have to do it from time to time. When you first start to clean out the closet, you pull out lots of stuff that has been crammed in there for a while. The bedroom gets messy with stuff sprawling out everywhere. You begin to wonder if you made a huge mistake opening this can of worms. But little by little you organize the clothes and other items. You sort through what you need to discard or donate and what you will keep. You find a better way to organize and store the items. Maybe you get new shelving that will accommodate your items in a much tidier manner. In the end, the room and closet are clean, it is much easier to

45

use, and you feel better about how you are storing things in your closet. But you know that if you don't keep things tidy on a consistent basis, you will have to eventually go through that process all over again.

Therapy is the place where you dig into issues, pull them out to examine, make choices about what to keep and what to discard, and organize your relationships in new ways that make things better and functional for all concerned. It is often hard and painful, but in the long-run it is worth it. So, if you are feeling a little pained or overwhelmed by therapy at this point in the process, don't worry. That's probably normal. Hang in there and continue working through these workbooks and working with your counselor. Working together for the love you both desire is hard work, but be optimistic. Tell yourself that you can do hard things and that your relationship is worth it. In the long-term, your relationship will be worth whatever investment of energy and effort the two of you collaborate together to put into it. Don't be dissuaded due to the difficulty. Don't give up.

One of my favorite quotes about facing difficult things comes from Dr. M. Scott Peck's book *The Road Less Travelled*. His book opens with the following quote:

"Life is difficult. This is a great truth, one of the greatest truths. It is a great truth because once we truly see this truth, we transcend it. Once we truly know that life is difficult – once we truly understand and accept it – then life is no longer difficult. Because once it is accepted, the fact that life is difficult no longer matters."

Talk with your therapist about the issues and challenges you are facing and seek practical solutions to those problems. The context of CAST gives you a framework to address the issues that are specific to you and your relationship. Think of CAST like a large toolbox with many tools, but you, your partner, and your therapist need to identify which tools would best help with which problems. This is a moment in the therapy process that your therapist and the two of you should ensure that you are all on the same page about what problems you are working on and what the treatment plan looks like as you move forward together.

COLLABORATING FOR CONNECTION AS A COUPLE

. . .

HOMEWORK – **Chapter 5: Therapy Treatment Planning**

This week your homework is a little easier than the previous one. In your next session ask you therapist to briefly summarize your treatment plan. Be sure that your therapist and each of you are all in agreement about what you need to work on and how you should be proceeding. Your therapist will likely have some suggested books, articles, or blogs pertaining to your specific issue or issues that they will suggest you read and discuss.

RECOMMENDED **Readings**

- Ask your therapist for book recommendations specific to your presenting problem(s).

CONTINUING THERAPY WITH COLLABORATIVE ATTACHMENT SYSTEMS THERAPY

Continue treatment with your therapist and the second workbook in the CAST model:

The *TRAIL to Love: Collaborative Attachment Systems Therapy Workbook 2 for Couples*

Available on Amazon

NOTES

INTRODUCTION

1. Weir, Kyle N. (2016). *Intimacy, Identity, and Ice Cream: Teaching Teens and Young Adults to Live the Law of Chastity*. Springville, UT: Cedar Fort Publishing.

1. CHAPTER ONE - PREPARATIONS: PAIRING WITH YOUR PERCEPTIONS (AND PAIRING AGAINST THE PROBLEMS)

1. Lambert, M. J., & Barley, D. E. (2001). Research summary on the therapeutic relationship and psychotherapy outcome. *Psychotherapy: Theory, Research, Practice, Training*, 38(4), 357–361.
2. See Catherall, D. R. (2007). Emotional safety: Viewing couples through the lens of affect. New York, NY: Routledge/Taylor & Francis Group.;
Butler, M. H., & Wampler, K. S. (1999). Couple-responsible therapy process: Positive proximal outcomes. Family Process, 38(1), 27–54.; and
Halford, W. K., Sanders, M. R., & Behrens, B. C. (1994). Self-regulation in behavioral couples' therapy. Behavior Therapy, 25(3), 431–452.
3. An early example of the concept of family systemic change through changing just one portion can be found in:
Watzlawick, P., Weakland, J.H., & Fisch, R. (1974; or 2011 Reprint Edition). *Change: Principles of problem formation and problem resolution*. New York, NY: W.W. Norton & Co.
Wile, D. B. (1978). Is a confrontational tone necessary in conjoint therapy? Journal of Marriage and Family Counseling, 4(3), 11–18.
And more recently in:
Franklin, C., Jordan, C., & Hopson, L. (2008). Intervention with families. In W. Rowe, L. A. Rapp-Paglicci, K. M. Sowers, & C. N. Dulmus (Eds.), *Comprehensive handbook of social work and social welfare, volume 3: Social work practice*. (pp. 423–446). Hoboken, NJ: John Wiley & Sons Inc.

2. CHAPTER TWO - COLLABORATION

1. Kilmann, R. H., & Thomas, K. W. (1977). Developing a forced-choice measure of conflict-handling behavior: The "MODE" instrument. *Educational and Psychological Measurement*, 37(2), 309–325.

NOTES

2. Gottman, J.M. (2011). *The science of trust: Emotional attunement for couples.* New York, NY: W.W. Norton & Co., p. 21.
3. See: Gottman, J. M., & Gottman, J. S. (2015). Gottman couple therapy. In A. S. Gurman, J. L. Lebow, & D. K. Snyder (Eds.), *Clinical handbook of couple therapy* (p. 129–157). The Guilford Press.
   Also: https://www.gottman.com/about/the-gottman-method/
4. Gottman, J.M & Silver, N. (2015). The *seven principles for making marriage work.* New York, NY: Three Rivers Press.
5. Broderick, C.B. (1979). *Couples: How to confront problems and maintain loving relationships.* New York, NY: Simon & Schuster, Inc.
6. Carlfred B. Broderick (1993). *Understanding Family Process: Basics of Family Systems Theory.* Newbury Park, CA: SAGE Publications, Inc.
7. William J. Doherty (2013). *Take Back Your Marriage: Sticking Together in a World That Pulls Us Apart,* 2nd edition. New York, NY: Guilford Press.

3. CHAPTER THREE - ATTACHMENT: THEORY

1. See https://oceanservice.noaa.gov/news/june15/sea-turtles.html
2. https://ourworldindata.org/child-mortality
3. * Note that parents do not need to be perfect to be consistent. "Inconsistency" does not mean the rare parental mistake that all parents make, occasionally. Rather, inconsistent parenting, is characterized by polar opposite experiences that the child does not know whether to trust the parent or not. Research shows that "good enough" parenting can build healthy attachments and that overemphasizing "perfect parenting" can actually leave the child anxious.
4. Sue Johnson (2013). *Love Sense: The Revolutionary New Science of Romantic Relationships.* New York, NY: Little, Brown and Company.
5. Sue Johnson (2008). *Hold Me Tight: Seven Conversations for a Lifetime of Love.* New York, NY: Little, Brown and Company.
6. Sue Johnson, Jim Furrow, Allison Lee, Gail Palmer, Doug Tilley, and Scott Woolley (2005). *Becoming an Emotionally Focused Couple Therapist: The Workbook.* New York, NY: Routledge/Taylor & Francis Group.
7. Ivan Boszormenyi-Nagy and Geraldine Spark (1984). *Invisible Loyalties,* New York, NY: Brunner-Mazel Publishers, p. xiv.

4. CHAPTER FOUR - SYSTEMS AS A WAY TO REBUILD RELATIONSHIPS

1. Watzlawick, P., Beavin, J.H., & Jackson, D.D. (1967), *Pragmatics of Human Communication,* W.W. Norton & Company, New York, p. 51.
2. Rosen, E. M., Weir, K., and Tracz, S. (2016). An innovative methodology for assessing student learning outcome achievement. CLEARvoz, 3(1), 14-25. – Published on-line Feb. 16, 2016.
3. Faber, A. J. (2002). The role of hierarchy in parental nurturance. American Journal of Family Therapy, 30(1), 73–84.

NOTES

4. Gottman, J.M & Silver, N. (2015). The *seven principles for making marriage work.* New York, NY: Three Rivers Press, pp. 26-27.
5. Gottman, J.M. (2011). *The science of trust: Emotional attunement for couples.* New York, NY: W.W. Norton & Co.

ABOUT THE AUTHOR

Kyle N. Weir, Ph.D., LMFT, is a Professor of Marriage, Family, and Child Counseling in the Counselor Education program at California State University—Fresno. He has also previously served as Chair of the Department of Counselor Education and Rehabilitation and as Coordinator of the Counselor Education program. He currently serves as the Associate Director of Fresno Family Counseling Center – a student-training clinic operated by the faculty and students of Fresno State's Marriage, Family, and Child Counseling degree serving the needs of the California Central Valley community. He primarily teaches the following courses: Couples Therapy, Family Therapy Theories, MFT Business Practices, and Advanced Practicum/Supervision courses. He received a B.S. in Public Policy and Management, an M.A. in Sociology (Organizations), a M.M.F.T. in Marital & Family Therapy, and a Ph.D. in Sociology/Marriage and Family Therapy from the University of Southern California. He is a licensed marriage and family therapist in California, was a part-time clinician at LDS Family Services, and now practices with the firm Roubicek & Thacker, Inc. He also serves as the Clinical Director of LifeSTAR of the Central Valley through Roubicek and Thacker, Inc.

He is married to Allison Brown Weir, and they have six children: Kellie, Nathan, Samantha, Joshua, Jason, and Daniel. It was through the personal adoption experiences with his children that Dr. Weir developed an academic interest in play therapy with adoptive and foster families.

He has also spent decades doing couples therapy, as well as supervising his students who engage in couples therapy. The Collaborative Attachment Systems Therapy model was developed through his academic teaching, supervision, and clinical experience with couples therapy. Dr. Weir is the author of numerous peer-reviewed journal articles and the books *Coming Out of the Adoptive Closet* (2003; University Press of America), *The Choice of a Lifetime: What You Need to Know Before Adopting* (2011; NTI Upstream), *Intimacy, Identity, and Ice Cream: Teaching Teens and Young Adults to Live the Law of Chastity* (2016; Cedar Fort Publishing); *Why Repentance Matters* (2018, Finegold Creek Press); and a forthcoming book *Saints Overcoming Scrupulosity*.

For more information visit:
www.drkyleweir.com

For clinical appointments or questions contact:
Kyle N. Weir, PhD, LMFT
Roubicek and Thacker, Inc. (Private Practice)
1879 E. Fir Ave., Suite 103, Fresno, CA 93720
559-323-8484
https://roubicekandthacker.com/individual-couples-family-counseling

Made in the USA
Coppell, TX
25 February 2025

46413000R00046